Stand Up Speak Out

A book about children's rights, written by young people around the world

Editors from the first meeting

Selda Altun, 15, U.K.
Zuhra Bahman, 18, Afghanistan
Gulizar Candemir, 15, U.K.
Carmen Jungblut, 14, Canada
Caireen McPhillips, 17, U.K.
Gyanu Sharma, 18, Nepal

Editors from the second meeting

Jabran Ali, 14, U.K.
Patricia Avalós, 18, Argentina
Charlotte Cowell, 16, U.K.
Himanshu Singh Dillon, 15, India
Vahakn Matossian Gehlhaar, 17, U.K.
Vahagn Hamalbashyan, 17, Armenia
Zoe Hawkins, 15, Canada
Marina Paradnya, 16, Belarus

The virtual editors

Tom Burke, 16, U.K.
Mihir Chatterjee, 16, India
Melanie Coulas, 16, Canada
Vaibhav Dayal, 15, India
Mudit Jaju, 16, India
Raghav Mathur, 16, India
Aleksandar Peshev, 16, Macedonia
Dana Shaddad, 17, Qatar
Ashish Suwal, 15, Nepal

The Peace Child team

Project Director and Senior Editor: Julian Olivier, U.K.
Project Co-ordinator: Rosey Simonds, U.K.
Project Administrator: Laura Arrieta Abellan, Costa Rica
Designer: Francisco Pereira, Ecuador
Educational Adviser: Susan Hawkins, Canada

Gyanu, Gulizar, Selda, Carmen, Zuhra, Caireen, Vahakn, Charlotte, Marina, Jabran, Vahagn, Himanshu, Patricia

Vaibhav, Aleksandar, Ashish, Dana, Raghav, Tom, Mudit, Melanie, Mihir, Laura, Julian, Susan, Francisco, Rosey, Zoe

'Bodies' by Jabran Ali, 14, U.K.

We would like to thank the following organizations for their generous support of this project: UNICEF (U.K.), Ben and Jerry's, Polden-Puckham Charitable Foundation and Amnesty International.

Thanks also to Nicole Toutounji, Hashi Roberts and Pat Lone from UNICEF, Heather Jarvis from UNICEF (UK), Elizabeth Gilbert from Survival, Frances Ellery and Sue Sneddon from Save the Children, Dan Jones and Stewart Coleman from Amnesty International, NSPCC, Intendente Municipal de Ezeiza (Argentina), Mr. and Mrs. Alejandro Granados, Empresa Constructora Altieri e Hijos (Argentina), Carolyne Willow, Don Harrison, Susan and Aaron Hawkins, Tom Jolly and David Woollcombe.

Peace Child International
Project Director and Senior Editor: Julian Olivier
Project Coordinator: Rosey Simonds
Project Administrator: Laura Arrieta Abellan
Designer: Francisco Pereira
Educational Adviser: Susan Hawkins

act-two
Editorial Director: Jane Wilsher
Project Manager: Deborah Kespert
Senior Designer: Lisa Nutt
Design Support: Judith Stevens
Editorial Support: Lucy Poddington

Front cover: Designed by Picthall and Gunzi

Created by **act-two** for Two-Can Publishing
First published in 2001 by Two-Can Publishing
A division of Zenith Entertainment plc
43–45 Dorset Street, London W1U 7NA

Dewey Decimal Classification 323
HC ISBN 1-58728-540-1
SC ISBN 1-58728-541-X

1 2 3 4 5 6 7 8 9 0 04 03 02

Printed in Hong Kong by Wing King Tong

Photographic credits
p.10 Ironbridge Gorge Museum Trust, Elton Collection (left), UN PHOTO 165054/Lois Conner (right), UN Photo 143686 (top), the United Nations (bottom); p.11 UNICEF/HQ90-0117/ RUBY MERA (top), UNICEF/HQ90-0102/ JOHN CHIASSON (bottom); p.14 UNICEF/HQ96-0591/ NICOLE TOUTOUNJI (right), UNICEF/HQ00-0250/ GIACOMO PIROZZI (bottom); p.15 UNICEF/HQ96-1166/ GIACOMO PIROZZI (left), UNICEF/HQ97-0331/ SHEHZAD NOORANI (bottom); p.18 Charlie Olivier; p.31 the United Nations; p.32 Julian Olivier; p.33 Alexander Woollcombe; p.34–35 Save the Children (all); p.43 Survival; p.49 Article 12 (all); p.50 Peace Child International (left and bottom); p.51 UNICEF; p.62 Alexander Woollcombe; p.66 Brooke Brinsky; p.73 ChildLine; p.74 Zuhra Bahman; p.76 The Railway Children; p.77 Casa Alianza (all); p.86–87 Amnesty International (all); p.94 Peace Child International (all).

Publisher's notes

This book represents a year's work by the young members of the Peace Child International network. They gathered facts, interviews, opinions, stories, poems, and photographs from young people all around the world. This intensely personal material was then pulled together by a group of young editors who asked questions about the issues covered and provided their own general editorial comment. The book offers you a fresh perspective and a commentary on the Convention on the Rights of the Child.

It's an excellent starting point for discussions about children's rights. Teachers will find ideas for action throughout the book plus a list of useful organizations to contact on pages 92–93.

The publishers have made every effort to verify the facts, but not all information could be substantiated, especially that given in personal accounts. The views of the contributors are not necessarily those of the publishers, the United Nations, or any other organization mentioned.

Contents

How Our Book Was Made...

This is the story of how this book was made. It all began at the U.K. (United Kingdom) offices of Peace Child, where the team both works and lives. Peace Child is an international organization working with young people.

1 A few years ago, Jules, Rosey and the Peace Child team made a book about human rights called *Stand Up for Your Rights*. It was so popular that they were asked to make another one about children's rights written, illustrated, and designed by young people.

2 Over many weeks, Jules prepared a workbook explaining how to take part in the project. He and Rosey asked schools and youth groups from all parts of the globe to send in stories, poems, paintings, and drawings.

3 Youth groups, such as this one in Costa Rica, received the workbooks and set to work putting together their material.

4 A few weeks later, the postwoman arrived carrying piles and piles of letters. There were so many contributions that they filled up Jules's entire bedroom and he had to sleep in the hall!

5 Six young editors from Afghanistan, Nepal, Canada and the U.K. were selected to go to the Peace Child headquarters. Their task was to choose the best contributions and produce a first draft of the book.

6 The team spent two long weeks preparing this draft. There were still holes to fill, so the draft was sent back to the youth groups for more ideas.

7 The next week, there was a mountain of mail on the doorstep. The letters were full of artwork, poems, and stories.

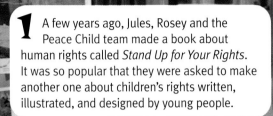

8 Next, a second editorial team of eight young people arrived to decide which stories, pictures, and poems would make it into the final book.

9b ...writing and editing

9c ...cooking

9d ...drawing

9a After a long brainstorming session, the team got busy...

9e ...and relaxing!

10 Laura organized a virtual editorial meeting so that people could send in stories and artwork via the Internet.

11 Jabran's mom worried so much about her son wasting away that she decided to make an enormous pot of spicy biryani for everyone.

12 The book was almost ready but the editors needed one last blast of inspiration so they headed off to London. Refreshed from their day out, they sat down for a final meeting.

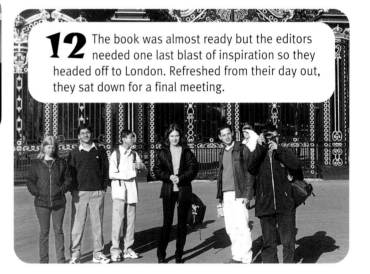

13 After the meeting, Francisco and the rest of the Peace Child team finished off the last missing pages.

14 Four weeks later, Julian handed over the pages to Deborah and Lisa at act-two. They made sure the pages were all looking perfect and got them ready for the printers. There, the pages were turned into printed books—one of which you are now reading!

Stand Up Speak Out

...We hope you enjoy our book.

Who made this book?

This book was made from stories, paintings, poems, drawings, and ideas sent in by the groups, schools, and individuals listed below.

North America 53

Central America

South America

12 · 16 · 19 · 15 · 41 · 14 · 9 · 42 · 7 · 13 · 2

1 Albania
Aquarius, Tirana

2 Argentina
Alejandro Velazquez E.E.M.
No3.-C Spegazzini
E.E.M. No.3 Tristán Suarez,
Buenos Aires
Esc. Educación Media No.3
Las Heras
Esc. Educación Media No.2
OEA, Buenos Aires
Escuela Núñez Francisco
Pazarelli
Instituto Maipú, Buenos Aires
IPEM No.50 Francisco Pazarelli,
Buenos Aires
Los PLANETARIOS, Tucumán
Los Verdecitos (PROFAUNA)
Laján, Buenos Aires
Mónica Jesús Herrera E.E.M.
No.2-C SpegazziniMisión
Peace Child, Argentina
Peace Child, Mendoza

3 Australia
CHAMPS Youth Project,
Murray Bridge, South Australia

4 Austria
5 BORG Schulschwestern
SOS Children's Village, Austria

5 Azerbaijan
Youth Development Organization,
Baku

6 Belarus
Club 'BEES', Minsk
Peace Child IFC Club, Gomel
Voices of Youth, Minsk

7 Bolivia
Hogar Marcelina, La Paz

8 Bosnia-Herzegovina
The First Bosniak High School,
Sarajevo

9 Brazil
Roberta Marques,
São Paulo

10 Cambodia
Khymer Youth,
Assoc. Phnom Penh

11 Cameroon
Rescue Mission Cameroon

12 Canada
Ernie Studer School,
Saskastchewan
Justine Hirschfeld
Rescue Mission Group at Spruce
Glen School, Ontario
Whycocomagh Cons, New Brunswick

13 Chile
Club Huemullín
Liceo Carlos Condell, Santiago
Pontifica Universidad, Santiago

14 Colombia
Children's Movement
Nueva Integración del Colombia

15 Costa Rica
Defensa de los Niños Internacional,
San José
Escuela de Arte Creatividad Infinita
Fundación Paniamor-Proyecto
Jóvenes, San José

16 Cuba
Escuelas José Martí, La Habana

17 Czech Republic
UNESCO Club, Olomouc

18 Democratic Republic of Congo
Assoc. p/l Defense
Ecole Africaine Kimbanguiste 12 Sept,
Kinshasa

19 El Salvador
CESTA, San
Salvador
Larissa Orellana,
San Salvador

20 France
Anita Conti Ecole
Publique
Collège Marcel
Carnée, Vineuil
Ecole 'Les Lucioles'
Médiatèque de
Saint-Avé

21 Ghana
Ashanti Goldfields Schools
Friends of the Nation
Green Earth Organization
Rescue Mission Ghana

22 Greece
Sevie Paida

23 Hong Kong
Committee on Children's
Rights
Ismile

24 India
Children's Rights in Goa
Mihir Chatterjee, Rajasthan
Mitesh Badiwala
M.S.M.S.V. School, Jaipur
PVCHR, Varanasi
Raghav Mathur, Rajasthan
Shanti Sadanam, Kerala
Shonali
Shrusti, Mah state
Springdales School, New Delhi

25 Indonesia
Eco Teens, Sukabumi

26 Ireland
The Irish Society for the Prevention
of Cruelty to Children

27 Israel
CARE
Peace Child Israel

28 Italy
Scuola Falcone, Milano

29 Japan
Mineko Okagami,
Sendai

30 Kenya
KURM,
Nairobi

31 Liberia
FOCUS,
Monrovia

32 Lithuania
Kaunas
Kalniecia
Secondary School

33 Macedonia
Atina Kajstorovska
First Children's Embassy in
the World
'Kole Nedelkovski' Primary
School

Madagascar
Groupe Ravinala

Malawi
Youth Net and Counselling, Zomba

Mali
Lassana Dounibia, Bamako

Malta
San Anton School

Nepal
Peace Child,
Nepal
Suyash Malla
Yangrima
School

Colegio Mariscal Caceres, Ayacucho
Colegio Teresa Gonzales de
Fanning, Lima
Comunidad Aguaruna, Cenepa,
Amazonas
Comunidad de Pillcopata, Cusco
Grupo Scout, Magdalena 34, Lima
Misión Rescate
Planeta Tierra
Varios
colegios,
Cusco

Uganda
Rescue Mission,
Uganda

U.K.
Article 12 Organization
Bahai Peacemaker Club,
Scotland

Vietnam
Thuy Anh

Yugoslavia
Stosic Roksalana

Zambia
Rescue Mision, Zambia

Europe

Asia

We'd like to say
a big thank you to
everybody who took
part in making
this book!

Africa

Philippines
Association of Children
of the Disappeared
Children and Peace,
Philippines
Friendship Garden School S.A.D.

Russia
Peace Child Krasnoyarsk

Rwanda
Facri Project Ssalongo
Mutesa Davis
Peace Child, Rwanda

Sierra Leone
Anthony Faux/Vamba Konneh

South Korea
Inchonjuone Primary School

Sri Lanka
Interactive Media Group , Kelaniya

Tanzania
Amani UNESCO Club

Casa Alianza,
U.K.
Freeman
College, Herts
Foyle Basin
Council, NI
George Mitchell School,
London
Lordship Farm School, Herts
St Christopher's School, Herts
St Mary's Catholic School, Herts
St Mary's School, Cambridge
Voice of Plymouth Schools

Ukraine
Peace Child Ukraine

U.S.A.
Brattleboro Union High School,
Vermont
Girls Incorporated, Dotham, Alabama
Indio High School, California
Marin County Day School,
California
Lick-Wilmerding High School,
California

Nigeria
LifeLink/
Rescue
Mission, Uyo

Pakistan
Pakistan
Environmental
Lobbying
Society, Lahore
Youth and
Development
Program,
Islamabad

Panamá
Nadia de Sedas, Panamá City

Peru
Albergue Infantil C.I.M.A, Lima
Asociación Filosófica Buho Rojo, Lima
Colegio Franco Peruano, Lima

Australia

What Is the C.R.C.?

C.R.C. stands for the Convention on the Rights of the Child. This is a document, set up by the United Nations, that officially gives rights to all children. It has been ratified, or agreed upon, by the leaders of every country in the world except for the U.S.A. and Somalia. This book tells you about the Convention and how it can affect children around the globe. The book is unique because it has been written and illustrated by young people. We hope you like it.

- On pages 10–11, we tell you a little about what the Convention is, why it was written, and what else has happened recently to improve children's rights.

- Next, there is an investigation into what different countries are doing to support the ideas in the Convention. In particular, we focus on UNICEF—the United Nations Children's Fund—which is an organization leading the way on children's rights.

- The chapter finishes with a timeline, taking you through key moments in history that have affected children and reflecting on what the future may hold.

Illustration by Andrea Bardusco, 11, Italy

How to use this book

How the book is divided up
The book is divided into chapters, each of which deals with a different set of articles from the Convention. At the start of each chapter, there is a panel with the words of the articles covered in that chapter.

Who wrote what?
Comments from the editors are written in **bold** or plain type and have no names alongside them. Quotes, poems, artwork, and stories from contributors are all credited.

Color coding
Each chapter is color coded (this chapter is yellow). On the edge of every page, you will see a colored strip showing the color for the chapter. This helps remind you which chapter you are reading. It also tells you which articles are being dealt with on that particular page.

If you don't understand something
If you can't find what you're looking for or there is a word you don't understand, just turn to our glossary and index on pages 95 and 96.

Journey to the Convention

This is the story of how the Convention on the Rights of the Child came about. Our research took us back to the Industrial Revolution in the 1800s, where it all began. This was a time when children had no rights at all.

The Industrial Revolution

During the 1800s in Europe and the U.S.A., new ways of working meant that more factories were being built. In Europe and the U.S.A., children were forced to operate machinery and work in mines, often for little money. Many people were appalled and tried to improve conditions for children. In the U.K. and U.S.A., laws were passed banning child labor.

▲ Small children were employed to work in the narrowest mines.

World War I

In 1914, World War I broke out. Many children died and others lost their parents. The horrors of the war made people realize how important it was to look after children. One of these people was Eglantyne Jebb. In 1919, she started an organization called Save the Children to help starving children in Europe.

The Declaration of the Rights of the Child

Eglantyne Jebb soon realized that an internationally agreed upon document was needed setting out the rights of children. So, in 1923, she wrote the Declaration of the Rights of the Child. The next year, governments from across the globe met in Switzerland and signed up to support the idea. Later, this Declaration became the basis for the Convention.

World War II

Between 1939 and 1945, millions of people died in World War II. Afterward, there was an international effort to build a new world based on freedom and equality. So in 1945, the United Nations (U.N.) was founded. The U.N. allows the world's governments to meet and discuss international concerns.

▲ This huge skyscraper in New York is the home of the U.N. headquarters.

The Declaration of Human Rights

In 1948, the U.N. agreed to the Universal Declaration of Human Rights which set out the rights for all people, not just children. It was written by a team headed by another heroine of human rights—Eleanor Roosevelt.

▲ Eleanor Roosevelt was the widow of the former president, Franklin D. Roosevelt. She was a great negotiator.

Pressure grows for a Convention on the Rights of the Child

After the signing of the Universal Declaration of Human Rights, organizations such as Save the Children campaigned to turn the Declaration of the Rights of the Child into a U.N. convention, or legal agreement. The United Nations Children's Fund (UNICEF) set up meetings to discuss what should be in the Convention. UNICEF is an agency of the U.N. which is entirely devoted to children.

Signing of the Convention

On November 20, 1989, the U.N. approved the Convention on the Rights of the Child. The Convention is more widely accepted than any other in the history of the U.N. An amazing 191 out of 193 countries have ratified, or agreed upon, the Convention.

fact

Did you know that 20th November is celebrated as "Child Rights Day" all over the world?

▲ The U.N. headquarters were transformed for the World Summit for Children. The heads of state sat in a large square so that they could all face each other.

The World Summit for Children

In September 1990, 71 heads of state met in New York for the first ever World Summit for Children. The aim of the summit was to improve the lives of all children.

▲ Candles were lit at the World Summit for Children along with one million others around the world.

The Special Session on Children

In September 2001, the U.N. General Assembly held a special session on children. Earlier in the year, the Global Movement for Children had been launched to raise awareness of the conditions of children around the world.

Convention countdown

1914 -1918 World War I: thousands of young people are killed and millions more are left homeless, orphaned, or wounded.

1919 Eglantyne Jebb and her sister, Dorothy Buxton, found Save the Children to protect starving children after the war.

1923 Eglantyne Jebb writes the Declaration of Child Rights which eventually forms the basis for the Convention.

1939 -1945 World War II: millions of children are killed and made homeless in Europe.

1945 The United Nations (U.N.) is set up by 50 countries to provide a place for debating international issues and resolving conflicts. Today, more than 180 countries and territories are members.

1946 The United Nations Children's Fund (UNICEF) is created to provide food, clothing and medicine for children affected by World War II.

1979 International Year of the Child: the decision is made to turn the Declaration into a full convention, enforceable by law.

1989 The Convention on the Rights of the Child is adopted by the U.N. General Assembly.

1990 World Summit for Children: 71 heads of state gather in New York. They agree upon a World Declaration on the survival, protection, and development of children.

1995 50th anniversary of the U.N.

2001 U.N. Special Session on Children: leaders meet to review what the Convention has achieved and create a plan for the future.

Thanks to UNICEF for supplying the information and statistics for these pages.

Convention Update

Once a country has ratified, or agreed to the Convention, it reports to the U.N. Committee on the Rights of the Child first after two years and then every five years to show how it has put the Convention into practice. Through this system, much has been done to improve the lives of children. Here are just a few things that have been achieved since the U.N. adopted the Convention on November 20, 1989:

" A century that began with children having virtually no rights has ended with children having the most powerful instrument that not only recognizes but also protects their human rights. "
Carol Bellamy, Executive Director, UNICEF, 1999

Every year in developing countries, over 100 million children are being immunized against diseases. This saves 2.5 million young lives per year.

In developing countries, 78% of people have access to improved drinking water.

Children's parliaments, forums, and councils have been set up all over the world.

Since 1988, the number of reported cases of polio worldwide has fallen by 99% to 3,500.

Using child soldiers is now an international war crime.

Between 1994 and 1996, South African children took part in drafting the new Constitution.

Illustration by Sandra Hoemí Córdoba, 14, Argentina

Flag illustrations opposite by Leanna Lugmayer, 15, U.K.

Thanks to UNICEF for supplying the information and statistics for these pages.

A country comparison

We decided to compare the situation for children in six different countries by looking at UNICEF's "State of the World's Children" reports for information and statistics. This is what we found.

ANGOLA, Africa

Population: 12.5 million
Under five mortality rate: 295 children in every 1,000 die before the age of five.
Literacy: 42 percent of people can read and write.
Good news:
Angola has now included the ideas in the Convention in the laws that govern the country.
Anything to note:
From the early 1960s until 1974, there was a war of independence against Portugal. Since then, a civil war has been tearing the country apart. About one million children cannot live in their own homes.

COSTA RICA, Central America

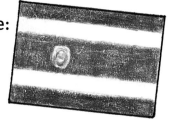

Population: 3.9 million
Under five mortality rate: 14 children in every 1,000 die before the age of five.
Literacy: 95 percent of people can read and write.
Good news:
Greater efforts are now being made to register newborn children.
Anything to note:
Costa Rica does not have an army.

BURKINA FASO, Africa

Population: 11.6 million
Under five mortality rate: 199 children in every 1,000 die before the age of five.
Literacy: 19 percent of people can read and write.
Good news:
Schools in Burkina Faso teach seven to nine year olds in their local language and give them training in life skills. This has resulted in more girls going to school, fewer dropouts, and more parents becoming involved with school activities.

U.S.A.

Population: 276 million
Under five mortality rate: Eight children in every 1,000 die before the age of five.
Literacy: 99 percent of people can read and write.
Anything to note:
The U.S.A. has not ratified the Convention. Many people feel that children's rights are respected in the U.S.A., so there is no need.

U.K.

Population: 58.7 million
Under five mortality rate: Six children in every 1,000 die before the age of five.
Literacy: 99 percent of people can read and write.
Good news:
Children in Wales now have a commissioner to make sure that their rights are respected. There are plans to do the same in Northern Ireland and Scotland.
Anything to note:
As yet, no decision for a children's commissioner in England has been made.

INDIA, Asia

Population: 1 billion
Under five mortality rate: 98 children in every 1,000 die before the age of five.
Literacy: 58 percent of people can read and write.
Good news:
In 1998, health workers and volunteers immunized 134 million children against polio.
Anything to note:
Child labor is an important issue here. Mudit Jaju, one of the editors, says, "Now the situation is a bit better because the government cracks down on companies and unions that use children."

unicef
United Nations Children's Fund

UNICEF is one of the organizations that helped encourage countries to adopt and ratify the Convention on the Rights of the Child. We asked UNICEF staff to tell us what they do.

FACT FILE

What is UNICEF? UNICEF stands for the United Nations Children's Fund. It is the only part of the U.N. that is dedicated to children.

What are its aims? UNICEF looks for solutions to the problems faced by poor children and their families. It also tries to give basic rights to all children.

What does it do? UNICEF sets up programmes and works with governments to help protect children's rights and meet their basic needs. Its projects include fighting discrimination, making childbirth safe, preventing childhood illnesses, and working with communities to ensure that girls as well as boys go to school.

Where does it carry out its work? UNICEF's headquarters are in New York and it has offices in 135 countries around the world. All together, UNICEF carries out work in 162 countries and territories.

" *The six billionth child born at the turn of the 20th century was more likely to have begun a life marked by malnutrition, inadequate or no schooling, poor sanitation, unsafe drinking water, gender discrimination and abuse. That child is endowed with fundamental human rights. Together we must build a global alliance to ensure those rights—in the knowledge that to serve the best interests of children, we serve the best interests of humanity.* "
Carol Bellamy, Executive Director, UNICEF

▲ A Syrian woman holds her baby. Today, all children in Syria are immunized against diseases. In addition, 90 percent of Syrian people have access to health services and 85 percent have safe drinking water.

UNICEF at work in Zambia

In Zambia, UNICEF helps communities to build and run village schools. Most children in villages are very poor, so they benefit from being able to go to a school nearby.

They cannot afford to travel long distances to and from school and cannot pay standard school fees. Many of the children are orphans. The teachers come from the local area as well.

▲ The Nthombimbi Elementary School water pump in action!

At Nthombimbi Elementary School, a community school in Zambia, UNICEF has paid for a water pump. Children at the school enjoy drinking and playing with clean water.

UNICEF SAVES LIVES

Now that you know a bit about UNICEF, let's take a look at some of the activities they are involved in.

Caring for children at each stage of life

UNICEF helps pregnant women to prepare for giving birth and to eat healthily. It also encourages breastfeeding as a way of providing the best nutrition for babies. For older children, UNICEF helps to set up schools. It supports young people by providing information about life skills and health care, including HIV and AIDS.

Providing clean water

Many children become ill or die because the water they drink and use is unsafe. UNICEF makes sure that more and more families have clean drinking water. As a result, the dangerous Guinea worm which enters into humans through contaminated water has almost been wiped out.

▲ In Mozambique, a woman holds her toddler son while a health worker gives him a dose of vitamin A. At this two-day immunization session, 5,000 people receive help.

UNICEF's key principles

UNICEF says that the easiest way to understand what the Convention is all about is to remember the four key principles:

SURVIVAL
DEVELOPMENT
PROTECTION
PARTICIPATION
of all children

Immunization

Every year, UNICEF helps save countless lives by immunizing 100 million babies against the six major childhood illnesses—diphtheria, measles, whooping cough, polio, tuberculosis, and tetanus. It costs about $14 to immunize one child.

Malaria

UNICEF provides mosquito nets that prevent people from catching malaria from mosquito bites. This can reduce child deaths by about one quarter.

Diarrhea

Children with diarrhea need medicine to avoid suffering from dehydration, or lack of water. Since 1990, child deaths from diarrhea have dropped by more than one-third thanks to UNICEF providing this medicine.

Nutrition

Many people become ill through malnutrition because their diets don't give them important vitamins. UNICEF gives out pills to overcome this.

Keeping children alive in Bangladesh

In Bangladesh, UNICEF supports a program to improve nutrition for 400,000 children and 500,000 pregnant mothers. It provides important vitamins and salts for children.

Most Bangladeshi people now have safe water. Children receive immunization tablets and injections, which means that many diseases are becoming less common.

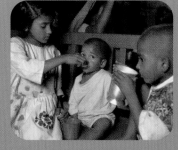

▲ A Bangladeshi child is given vital medicine.

Bangladesh also has many community schools. But despite this, 68 percent of children still don't eat enough food or receive the necessary vitamins to keep them healthy.

Thanks to UNICEF for supplying the information and statistics for these pages.

A Child Rights Journey ... the Past

Imagine you could step into a time machine and visit the most important events in the history of children's rights. What do you think you would find? This is our journey.

START HERE

Ancient Times

Killing baby girls
In some parts of the world, parents used to prefer to have male children. A habit arose of killing baby girls.

551–479 B.C. Confucius
The Chinese philosopher Confucius is believed to have set up the first formal school for children.

Slavery
Since ancient times, adults and children have been sold as slaves and forced to work.

1900–1950

1939–1945 The Holocaust
In Europe, six million Jews were murdered. More than 1.5 million of them were children.

1918–1919 The influenza epidemic
A worldwide outbreak of flu killed more people (especially children) than all the soldiers who died in World War I.

1910 Abolition of slavery in China
The end of slavery in China meant freedom for millions of children and their families.

1939–1945 Evacuees
During World War II, millions of children had to leave home. Many of them were taken to other countries and some never found their parents again.

1946 UNICEF
The United Nations Children's Fund (UNICEF) was set up to help young victims of World War II.

1948 The start of apartheid
In South Africa, the apartheid system separated "Blacks" from "Whites." Black children had very few rights. Apartheid ended in 1991.

1950–2000

1960s Cultural revolution
In the 1960s, young people developed their own fashion and culture. Musicians, such as The Beatles, showed them how they could build their own identities.

Thanks to The Imperial War Museum for supplying statistics about the Holocaust.

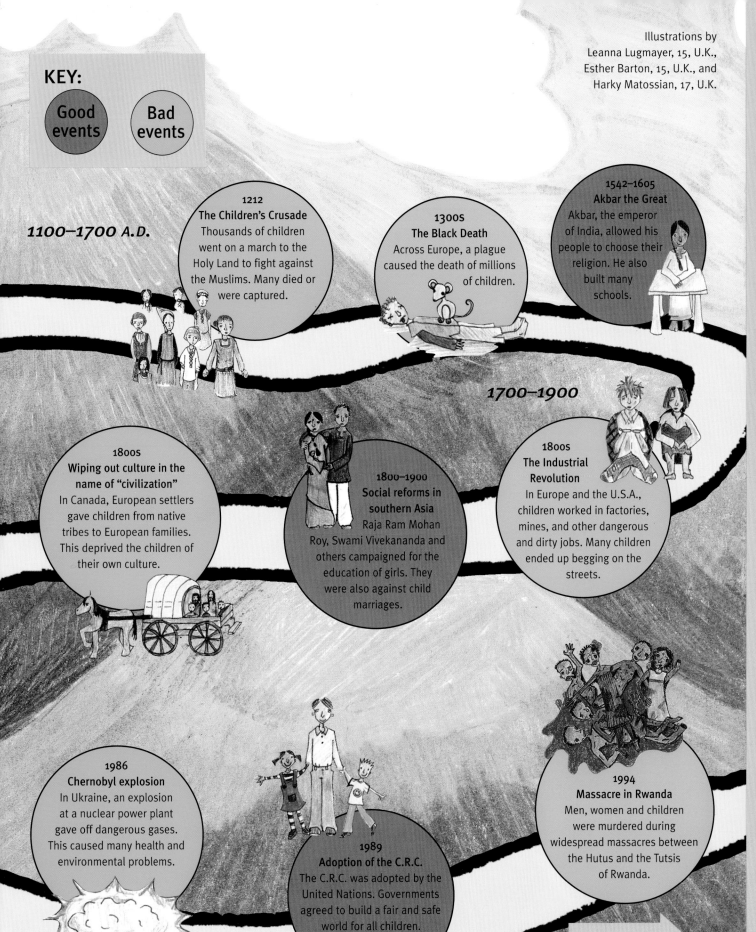

Illustrations by
Leanna Lugmayer, 15, U.K.,
Esther Barton, 15, U.K., and
Harky Matossian, 17, U.K.

KEY:

Good events

Bad events

1100–1700 A.D.

1212
The Children's Crusade
Thousands of children went on a march to the Holy Land to fight against the Muslims. Many died or were captured.

1300s
The Black Death
Across Europe, a plague caused the death of millions of children.

1542–1605
Akbar the Great
Akbar, the emperor of India, allowed his people to choose their religion. He also built many schools.

1700–1900

1800s
Wiping out culture in the name of "civilization"
In Canada, European settlers gave children from native tribes to European families. This deprived the children of their own culture.

1800–1900
Social reforms in southern Asia
Raja Ram Mohan Roy, Swami Vivekananda and others campaigned for the education of girls. They were also against child marriages.

1800s
The Industrial Revolution
In Europe and the U.S.A., children worked in factories, mines, and other dangerous and dirty jobs. Many children ended up begging on the streets.

1986
Chernobyl explosion
In Ukraine, an explosion at a nuclear power plant gave off dangerous gases. This caused many health and environmental problems.

1989
Adoption of the C.R.C.
The C.R.C. was adopted by the United Nations. Governments agreed to build a fair and safe world for all children. The U.S.A. did not sign the C.R.C.

1994
Massacre in Rwanda
Men, women and children were murdered during widespread massacres between the Hutus and the Tutsis of Rwanda.

TURN PAGE →

A Child Rights Journey ... the Future

Back in the present day, we took out the magnifying glass to find out what's going on here and now. Then we tried to imagine what we would see if we could time travel into the future...

2001 Child labor
In most developing countries, children work in factories or in places where their health is constantly at risk.

2001 HIV/AIDS
The HIV/AIDS virus has already infected about 10 million children. In Africa, 9 million children have been orphaned by the virus.

2001 Child soldiers
All over the world, child soldiers are made to fight wars that they had no part in starting.

CHILD SLAVES

2001 Camel jockeys
In parts of Asia, child slaves are strapped on to camels and forced to race. About one-third of the child jockeys die every year.

Now you are faced with a choice. Which future will you choose?

A future which ignores abuses of children's rights?

A future where children's rights are fully respected?

2001 Globalization
Rapid advancements in technology along with the tireless efforts of many organizations are bringing our world closer together.

2001 Education
The situation is improving. In developing countries, 90 percent of children enrol in a school, although only 68 percent complete the first four years.

MATHS

2001 The Paralympics
The Paralympics are held alongside the Olympics. They make people aware of the rights of people with disabilities, as well as inspiring disabled children to make the most of their futures.

Thanks to UNICEF for supplying the statistics for this page.

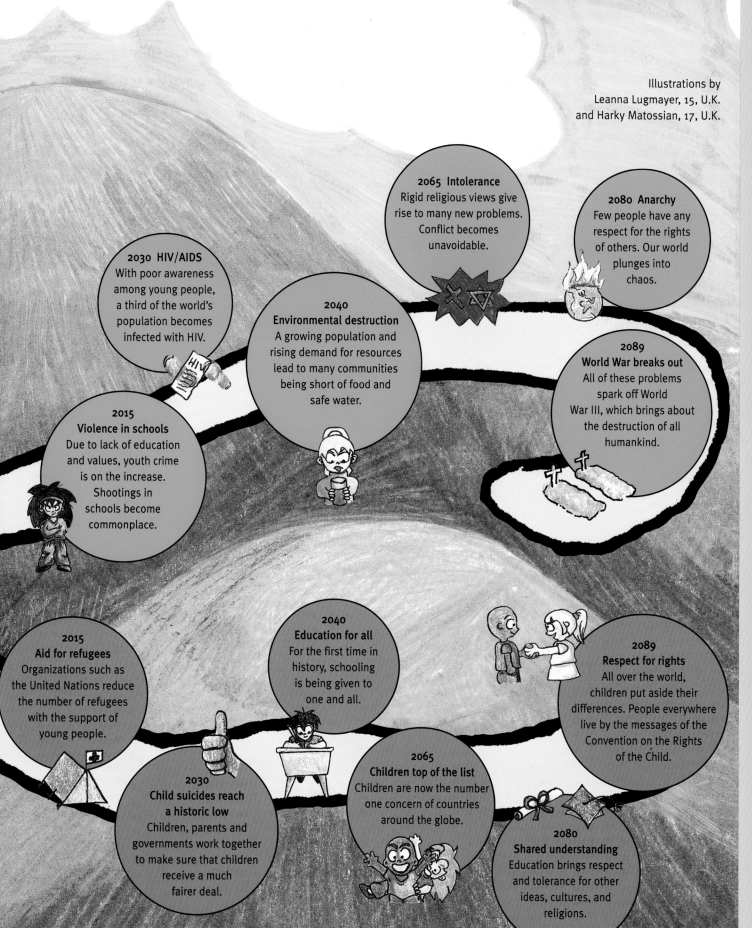

Illustrations by
Leanna Lugmayer, 15, U.K.
and Harky Matossian, 17, U.K.

2065 Intolerance
Rigid religious views give rise to many new problems. Conflict becomes unavoidable.

2080 Anarchy
Few people have any respect for the rights of others. Our world plunges into chaos.

2030 HIV/AIDS
With poor awareness among young people, a third of the world's population becomes infected with HIV.

2040
Environmental destruction
A growing population and rising demand for resources lead to many communities being short of food and safe water.

2089
World War breaks out
All of these problems spark off World War III, which brings about the destruction of all humankind.

2015
Violence in schools
Due to lack of education and values, youth crime is on the increase. Shootings in schools become commonplace.

2015
Aid for refugees
Organizations such as the United Nations reduce the number of refugees with the support of young people.

2040
Education for all
For the first time in history, schooling is being given to one and all.

2089
Respect for rights
All over the world, children put aside their differences. People everywhere live by the messages of the Convention on the Rights of the Child.

2030
Child suicides reach a historic low
Children, parents and governments work together to make sure that children receive a much fairer deal.

2065
Children top of the list
Children are now the number one concern of countries around the globe.

2080
Shared understanding
Education brings respect and tolerance for other ideas, cultures, and religions.

19

Principles

There are 54 articles in the Convention on the Rights of the Child. Each chapter of this book deals with a different group of articles. This chapter looks at the first five articles (see below). These are the guiding principles behind the Convention and they deal with topics such as equality and responsibility.

● The idea of equality is featured on pages 22–23. Article 2 says that everyone should enjoy the rights in the Convention. It doesn't matter who you are, where you're from or what you look like.

● Pages 24–25 look at responsibility. Who is responsible for making sure that we have rights? The answer is, we all are and we should all make sure that other people enjoy their rights too.

● On pages 26–27, we think about whether people always act "in the best interests of the child." Check out the picture on the opposite page. It shows how children can end up being pawns in an adult "game of chess."

"Everyone's equal" by Anisia Pisani, 12, Italy

Articles in this chapter

Article 1
The Convention defines a child as a person under 18 unless national law recognizes that the age of majority is reached earlier.

Article 2
All the rights laid down in the Convention are to be enjoyed by children regardless of race, color, sex, language, religion, political or other opinion, national, ethnic or social origin, property, disability, birth, or other status.

Article 3
All actions concerning the child should be in her/his best interests.

Article 4
The country has an obligation to translate the rights of the Convention into reality.

Article 5
The country should respect the rights and responsibilities of parents to provide guidance appropriate to the child's capacities.

Illustration opposite by Karl Ellis, 17, U.K.

We Are All Equal

Although the Convention says that children should have the same rights no matter where they come from, what language they speak or what sex they are, this is often not the case. We've heard about several types of discrimination that still occur.

Racial discrimination

Have you heard of people getting jobs just because they belong to a particular racial group? Or, maybe you know about families who are unfairly treated because of the country they come from? We want to change this.

Religious equality

Throughout history, religion has been a positive factor but also the cause of terrible conflict. Even today, people are killed and children are turned away from school because they belong to a particular religion.

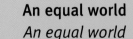

An equal world

*An equal world
Is where blacks and whites live together in
A peaceful and respectful environment.
An equal world
Is where there is an exchange of respect
Between the young and the old.
An equal world
Is where the strong cannot bully the weak.
An equal world
Is where rich and poor have dinner.
An equal world
Is where the high cannot use his position
To relegate the low to the background.
An equal world
Is where males regard females as capable
As men.*

Poem and illustrations by Carmen Jungblut, 14, Canada

Illustrations by Vahagn Hamalbashyan, 17, Armenia

Buddhist **Jew** **Muslim** **Hindu** **Christian**

> " *All of the different religions and faiths, despite their philosophical differences, have a similar objective. Every religion emphasizes human improvement, love, respect for others, and sharing other people's suffering.* " Dalai Lama, leader of the Tibetan Buddhists

Girls and boys—why aren't they equal?

The Convention says that there should be equality between girls and boys. But despite laws being passed, girls are still discriminated against in some way or another in nearly every country in the world.

Did you know that girls who receive at least four years of elementary education are likely to have healthier children and fewer children? That's why it's important to educate girls.
Caroline Smith, 16, U.S.A.

Illustration by
Patricia Avalós,
18, Argentina

Boys versus girls

Many parents are really disappointed when their baby turns out to be a girl. Why do you think this happens?
● Is it because boys can do more hard labor than girls?
● Is it because of religious beliefs?
● Is it because in many societies, property and money can only be inherited by males?

❝ Why does my father spend money on alcohol every day? He won't spend one paisa on my education. Is it because I am a girl? Don't girls have a right to education? To go to school? Or are we to spend the rest of our lives cooking, washing, and cleaning?❞

Parboti Tudia, 12, India

Rich and poor

Probably the biggest factor affecting whether or not you receive your rights is how rich your family is. As time goes on, the gap between those who have plenty and those who have little is getting wider. In your country, do the rich have more rights than the poor? If so, which rights are they, and why?

fact
More than one billion people live in poverty. Nine-tenths of them live in the developing world.

Illustration by Tanya Erzinclioglu, 14, U.K.

Thanks to UNICEF for supplying the statistics for this page.

Whose Responsibility Is It?

Article 4 gives the overall responsibility for enforcing the Convention to governments. However, we believe that there are other people who should be responsible too. Together, everyone can form an umbrella of protection for children.

Individuals

Each of us has a huge responsibility. We must be honest, show respect, and look out for others. If we feel that our rights or another child's rights are being broken, we shouldn't be afraid to speak out. Everyone has their part to play in improving children's rights.

Parents have rights too!

Article 5 gives parents the right and responsibility to give children the guidance they need. It asks the government to respect this right and we should too!

Illustration by Barbara Rodriguez, 9, Cuba

The State

Many governments say that they can't afford to provide medical care, education, or protection for children, but they can still find money to buy tanks and guns. Although it is true to say that the children of today are the adults of tomorrow, they are equally valuable for what they are today. Children are important.

Parents

Parents must ensure that every child feels loved and cared for. Even just listening to a child can change her or his life. Parents should treat their children fairly and with kindness.

Schools

Schools need to create an atmosphere where everyone's rights are respected and children are involved in decision making. Teachers must make sure that children are not bullied. They should also keep their eyes open to see that their pupils are being treated fairly.

Illustration by Marina Paradnya, 16, Belarus

Balancing Act

Children need rights but they have responsibilities, too. For example, you should have the right to express your views but that doesn't mean you can shout and cause trouble in your classroom. If you do this, you are depriving your classmates of their right to an education. It's all about balance. You should always respect other people's rights and feelings, at home, at school or in the playground.

Where?
Where have all the children gone?
They have been pushed into adulthood.
Where have all the scampering feet gone?
They have run as far as they could.
Where has all the happiness gone?
It has been stolen, as we knew it would.

Katie Paroschy, 14, Canada

fact

In the U.S.A. each state says when you can get married or drive. Everyone can vote at age 18.

Illustration by Marina Paradnya, 16, Belarus

When does a child become an adult?
Article 1 says a child is anyone under the age of 18. Each country has its own laws about when you are ready to drive, get married, vote, and work. But does having the right to vote or drive make you an adult? What would your definition of a child be?

Not allowed to grow up?
Do you ever feel that you're not being allowed to grow up? Children are often so protected from the outside world that they aren't prepared when they finally reach it. After all, if you aren't allowed to cross the street, you'll never learn about traffic, and if you never go to school on your own, how will you learn to do things for yourself? It's just a question of balance.

"Growing up" by Srijana Shrestha, 17, Nepal

It's Your Move

When we were writing this page, a few of us came up with the idea that life is often like a game of chess in which children are treated as pawns. On our chessboard, each piece represents a different type of person. They should all be acting in the best interests of the child but, as you can see, this doesn't always happen.

▶ Some parents use their children to achieve their own ambitions.

King

▲ Bad governments often neglect children's needs.

Castle

◀ Religion can be used to stir up racism and intolerance.

Bishop

Knight

▲ In some countries, police harass children they don't like.

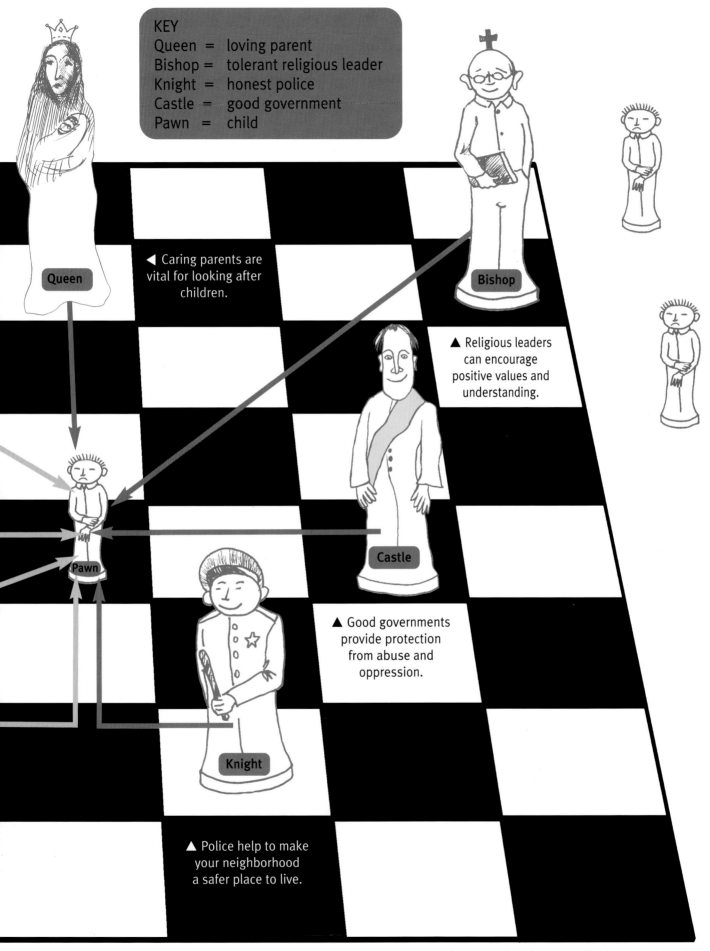

KEY
Queen = loving parent
Bishop = tolerant religious leader
Knight = honest police
Castle = good government
Pawn = child

◄ Caring parents are vital for looking after children.

▲ Religious leaders can encourage positive values and understanding.

▲ Good governments provide protection from abuse and oppression.

▲ Police help to make your neighborhood a safer place to live.

Illustrations by Vahagn Hamalbashyan, 17, Armenia

Your Rights as a Person

We all thought it would be a good idea to look at the rights that are essential to your life—the rights that give you life, help to make sure you stay alive, and the rights that tell you who you are. If you read the articles in the box below, you will soon realize that these are probably the most important rights of all.

- We start with the right to life, featuring a newspaper update on the biggest threats to children. Top of our list is the threat of AIDS.

- Next up, on pages 32–33, is a chance to think about all the things you just can't live without.

- On pages 34–35, we find out about Save the Children and how this organization is helping to improve children's lives.

- The chapter ends with stories of children who have lost their identities.

Illustration by Ira Bartnovskay, 15, Belarus

Articles in this chapter

Article 6 The right to life.

Article 7 The right to a name and a nationality and, as far as possible, the right to know and to be cared for by her/his parents.

Article 8 The right to protection of her/his identity by the country.

Article 24 The right to the highest standard of health and medical care attainable.

Article 26 The right to benefit from social security.

Article 27 The right to a standard of living adequate for her/his physical, mental, spiritual, moral, and social development.

C.R.C. TIMES

TUESDAY NOVEMBER 20, 2001

Who Are the Child Killers?

The right to life is the most precious right of all. It's also the biggest lottery. Your chances of survival depend on where you are born and what kind of medical treatment you have. The difference between life and death can hang on something as simple as a little pack of oral rehydration salts, costing just ten cents. Every year, oral rehydration salts save the lives of more than one million children, who would otherwise die from the effects of diarrhea.

Poverty

In poor countries, almost 30 percent of people live on less than one dollar per day. In rich countries too, one in every ten children lives below the poverty line. People living in poverty are far more likely to catch diseases. This year alone, more than 12 million children under five will die from poverty-related illnesseses.

Landmines

Every year, between 8,000 and 10,000 children are killed or injured by landmines.

In 1999, 4.1 babies were born every second. That's 129,384,000 per year – but how many survive?

Illustrations top and bottom by Jack Ridley, 15, U.S.A.

Violence & War

Conflicts used to involve people in battlefields. Today, 90 percent of the victims are civilians, mostly children. During the 1990s, about two million children were killed.

Malnutrition

About 183 million children under the age of five in the developing world do not get enough food. They need a good balance of foods to stay healthy.

Sickness

It would cost $10 trillion a year to effectively fight AIDS, malaria and tuberculosis. If every person living in rich countries gave $10, that total would be reached.

Saving Lives—the Good News

Around the world, more than 100 million babies per year are vaccinated against diseases such as diptheria, tetanus, whooping cough, polio, measles, and tuberculosis. This saves 2.5 million children each year.

Smallpox

Smallpox was stamped out 20 years ago.

Hospitals make a huge impact in helping to give children the right to life.

Polio

Polio was once a worldwide killer. In just 12 years, it has been nearly wiped out.

Blindness

Blindness due to lack of vitamin A has been reduced. However, 2.5 million children still lose their sight each year.

Measles

This killer disease has been reduced by 85 percent over the past ten years.

Thanks to UNICEF and "Children First" magazine for supplying the statistics for these pages.

"C.R.C. Times Logo" by Leanna Lugmayer, 15, U.K

HIV—Millions of Children at Risk

The World Health Organization says that 17 million people worldwide are infected with HIV. Although this is a problem that affects people everywhere, the greatest number of victims are found in sub-Saharan Africa (south of the Sahara desert). In Zimbabwe, AIDS kills 1,700 people every week. There will soon be 13 million children orphaned because of AIDS. At a recent meeting to discuss AIDS, Nelson Mandela was shocked to hear that half of all South Africans under the age of 15 will eventually die from AIDS.

In Zambia, a fifth of people are HIV positive. Just imagine if one in every five of your classmates were going to die of AIDS.

Illustration by Arokpa, 17, Benin

Kofi Annan's Warning

Kofi Annan

Kofi Annan, the Secretary-General of the United Nations, said, "Shame will fall upon the earth if we turn our backs on those affected by AIDS and cast them into the shadows. Time is not on our side but by acting now and by acting together we will make a difference."

AIDS and the Family

What happens when parents in Africa die of AIDS? Children often have to fend for themselves, trying to find food and looking after their younger brothers and sisters. There's no money for school fees or uniforms. The children worry about the reaction of other students and often drop out of school. Relatives might take over the house, leaving the children with no home and no one to provide for them. The more fortunate children get taken in by relatives or adopted but others end up living on the streets.

What Can Be Done?

People need to recognize that this is an emergency. Mothers with HIV can be treated with safe, effective drugs to stop the virus from spreading to their children. Schools should teach children about the dangers of AIDS. This can make a real difference: in Uganda, the government has cut the number of people infected by three-quarters just by educating people about the disease. Wealthier countries can offer more help to poorer countries so that they can educate people and fight poverty.

AIDS and School

860,000 elementary school children in Africa have lost their teachers because of AIDS—they either have caught the virus or they have to look after their relatives. AIDS affects schools in other ways, too. Money that would have been spent on improving schools is needed to cope with the effects of AIDS instead. Yet at school, children can get vital information about AIDS.

AIDS and Relatives

Freda heads a women's organization in Kenya. Her children are grown up so she has been devoting all her time to her work. Recently she came back from a conference to find that her sister-in-law had died leaving four orphaned children. She now has to start all over again raising children and paying school fees. She has no choice because there is no one else to help out.

Girls and AIDS

Young girls are more likely than boys to catch the virus. In South Africa, one in four females aged 15–24 is infected. It is crucial that young people are given more information. But if there is not enough money to educate children, boys are the ones sent to school in preference to girls.

Plan for the Future

Often, children whose parents die of AIDS don't receive their parents' property. In Uganda, special organizations help parents to appoint guardians and to write wills. This means that their children will receive their property instead of other relatives. The organizations also give parents the chance to create photograph albums to enable children to remember their parents and family. Support and counseling are on hand for the children as well as their parents.

A Decent Standard of Living

If you were to make a list of all the things you needed for a decent standard of living, what would be on it? This is our list. Imagine what your life would be like if you had...

NO house
You need a home where you feel safe.

NO school
Nearly 130 million children around the world don't go to school, two-thirds of whom are girls. With no education, it's harder to find a well-paid job and you are more likely to end up poorer than people who went to school.

NO food
Everyone needs healthy food. If you don't have a healthy and balanced diet, you risk catching diseases and becoming seriously ill.

NO safe water
Water must be safe for drinking, washing, and cooking. If you have to fetch water from a well, it needs to be within easy walking distance. In some places, poor people pay more for their water. They have to buy water from trucks while rich people have it piped into their homes.

NO space to play
Space and freedom to play make you feel happy.

NO doctor
If you are ill, you have the right to see a doctor and receive medicine and treatment. You need a clean home and immunization to help keep you healthy. Mothers and babies need special care and attention.

NO healthy environment
Breathing in dirty air can make you ill. The streets should be clean and the sewers must be properly maintained.

NO social security
When parents are unable to work, the family must not starve. There should be social security to provide money for food, clothes, shelter, and medicine.

NO safe streets
The streets need to be safe for walking around. You should be able to live without the fear of crime.

Thanks to UNICEF for supplying the statistics for this page.

Illustration by Rashmi Tuladhar, 13, India

ACTION idea

Make the change

It doesn't matter where you are from, poverty is all around us. If you want to make a difference, this is what you can do:

- Work from the top down. It is really important that you vote once you are old enough. Aim to elect governments and leaders who put the needs of children first.

- Work from the bottom up. Write to your local newspapers and youth magazines about making children's issues a priority.

- In your school assemblies, raise awareness about poverty in this country and abroad.

- Support organizations that improve the living conditions of those in need.

- Join a youth group to get your voice heard and acted on by local decision makers.

- Read the newspapers and surf the Internet to find out what is happening around you.

- Talk to your family or the people you live with about children's rights.

RECIPE:
How to change
a child's life

1 cup of youthful minds
2 tbsp. of vision
4 tsp. of motivation
½ cup of courage
A pinch of determination
to make a difference

Stir.
Serve immediately.
If neglected it will spoil.

* If you top this creation with amusement and entertainment, it is sure to be a success among all.

Recipe and illustration by Becky Carling, 14, Canada

HAIL TO THE CHEF!!

" *Even though the poverty you see in the U.K. looks different from the poverty you find in an African village, the causes of poverty are the same.* "

Tom Burke, 16, U.K.

Illustration by Nzuzi Matenkadi Giresse, 16, Democratic Republic of Congo

In this chapter, you have read about all kinds of difficult situations faced by children around the world. You may be wondering what anyone is doing about it. Well, there are many organizations working to improve children's lives. We found out more about Save the Children, which is at the front line in making the Convention become a reality.

What is Save the Children? Save the Children is an organization that works to protect children. It is part of an international group made up of 30 separate organizations. Together, they form the largest independent movement for children in the world.

What are its goals? Save the Children promotes children's rights. It aims to make immediate and lasting improvements to the lives of children around the world.

What does it do? When children are living in extreme poverty or caught up in emergencies such as earthquakes, Save the Children steps in. It works to make sure children stay alive and that their basic rights are respected. Save the Children supports the Convention on the Rights of the Child by writing to governments about it and by running educational programs to make the general public aware about child rights and how many children suffer from violence.

Where does it carry out its work? Save the Children operates in more than 100 countries.

◀ In Vietnam, Save the Children has set up a teacher training program where children can learn about health issues.

Eglantyne Jebb and the history of Save the Children

▲ Eglantyne Jebb, founder of Save the Children.

Eglantyne Jebb was born in Shropshire, U.K., in 1876. She was a brave and determined woman. Her work was vital in starting the movement to make sure that children have rights.

In 1913, Eglantyne went to the Balkans (former Yugoslavia) to join a relief mission. She helped child refugees affected by the Balkan War and was shocked by the conditions she saw.

At the end of World War I, in 1918, millions of children were dying of hunger and disease. So Eglantyne and her sister Dorothy founded Save the Children.

A CLOSER LOOK AT THE WORK

Save the Children has various programs that directly help children and their families, as well as focusing the world's attention on the rights of children.

Emergency relief

In times of war or during natural disasters, Save the Children is usually one of the first organizations on the scene. It provides medicine, shelter, and food for children in refugee camps. It also sets up family tracing programmes to reunite lost children with their families.

▼ Save the Children helps Kosovar refugee children in Macedonia find their parents.

▲ After a hurricane in Honduras, Save the Children gives out medical aid.

Speaking out

Save the Children has first-hand knowledge of where and how children's rights are being ignored. It does a great job of finding out where there is a problem and persuading the decision-makers to actually do something about it. On top of this, Save the Children joins forces with television stations and newspapers to tell the public about important issues.

Long term programs

Save the Children also has many long term programs which tackle issues such as health, food and nutrition, disability, child labor, gender discrimination, and HIV and AIDS.

▲ Save the Children trains staff members at a day care center in the Philippines.

▼ Young blind children in Ethiopia are helped to attend local schools.

Education

Education for children and adults alike is vital. Save the Children trains teachers, produces educational materials, and sets up schools for children who are missing out on an education.

▼ In rural Peru, students learn at a school supported by Save the Children.

▲ Tibetan refugee children are taught in special schools in refugee camps.

Before long, Eglantyne realized that it was not enough simply to send money, food, and medical supplies. Doctors and nurses had to be on hand to give expert assistance.

▲ Russian children receive food during a famine in 1919.

During the late 1920s, the situation in Europe started to improve. Eglantyne Jebb and Save the Children were able to offer help to children in other parts of the world as well.

Eglantyne Jebb died in 1928, aged 52. Her ideas continue to improve the lives of children worldwide through the work of Save the Children and its partners.

Thanks to Save the Children for supplying the information for these pages.

Who Are You?

The Convention gives you the right to a name, an identity and a nationality. Think how difficult life would be if you had no name, you didn't know where you were from and you weren't officially registered at birth. You would become a "nobody."

Interview with Laura

If you lose your parents when you are very young, you can grow up not knowing who you are. In Argentina, in the 1970s, political opponents of the military dictatorship sometimes "disappeared." They were put in jail or murdered. Their children were often given to families who supported the dictatorship. Walter Daniel Ojeda (17) and Alejandro Velasquez (18) interviewed Laura to find out her story.

Walter: What happened to your parents?

Laura: My father and mother met while working in the Peronist Army Forces. On August 4, 1979, my parents, sister, and I were running away to La Plata, but a car intercepted us. Soldiers dressed as civilians took away my parents and left my sister, aged four, and me, aged 11 months, in a corner. My mother shouted out an address and someone took us to my grandparents' house. Four days later, my father was killed. My mother and uncles "disappeared."

Alejandro: So who looked after you?

Laura: I had my grandparents. Other children were not so lucky. They were given to families who supported the dictatorship and never knew who their real families were at all. That is why we started the organization called HIJOS—Children for Identification and Justice against Forgetfulness and Silence.

Success story

UNICEF and registering births

Imagine not knowing when your birthday is! Each year, about 40 million children are not officially registered at birth. Without birth certificates, children's rights can easily be abused. In Bangladesh, UNICEF launched a massive campaign to encourage parents to register their children. In ten days, 2,500 volunteers visited 900,000 homes. They helped 100,000 babies become registered. Stickers like the one on the right were put on the doors of all the homes where babies had been registered.

Illustration by Patricia Avalós, 18, Argentina

Stolen: Aborigines in Australia

One of the editors, Zuhra, went to see an Australian play called *Stolen*. The play tells the story of five young Aboriginal children who were taken from their families and placed in a home. Many of the actors were Koori Aborigines who themselves had been "stolen." Zuhra learned that between 1910 and the mid 1970s, the Australian government decided to integrate Aborigines with white Australians. They started a practice where babies and children were "stolen" from their parents and taken to children's homes. They had no more contact with their families. The lighter-skinned Aborigines were adopted by white families, while the darker ones became domestic servants. One in every ten Aboriginal children was treated in this way. Having your culture and identity taken away from you means that you don't know where you're from. Once it has happened, there's usually no way back.

What children need:
encouragement, love,
respect, kindness,
and consistency.

What children don't need:
impatience, cruelty,
beatings, swearing,
and humiliation.

It's not fair!

The old always envy the world of children;
They think our world is full of fun,
But this is not always so,
For when a child breaks a glass
He is going to get a scolding;
When a child gets to bed late,
He is sure to get a rebuke;
When a child does not perform very well in school,
He is sure to get a talking to.
But when a father breaks a glass,
Mother only says, "Well..."
And when father gets his spelling wrong,
Mother only says, "It's due to tiredness."
So you see, the world of children is not
Always full of fun,
For we never have a good
reason for our mistakes.

Collins Abassah, 18, Ghana

Illustration by
Marina Paradnya,
16, Belarus

What Arrived in the Mail

While we were making this book, we received many letters about the difficulties that arise out of family situations. Maintaining a good relationship with your family is not always easy, as these letters and pictures show.

Don't be angry with m – I need love

Mika Kawauchi, 18, Japan

I was glad when my parents divorced. Sitting there and listening to their arguments every day made me very miserable. It was a huge relief when they finally decided on a divorce.

Yours,
Drew, 14, U.S.A.

Peace Child International
The White House
Buntingfor
Herts, SG9
UNITED KI

When I was four, my parents divorced and my dad left home. I still saw him every weekend, but it wasn't the same. Then my mum got a new boyfriend, Martin. He was a control freak. As time went on, we had many arguments. My mum never stuck up for me, which was really upsetting as I felt I couldn't talk to her about anything. After a year and a half of this, I made up my mind to move to my dad's. Martin said that I couldn't go. I was prepared to go into a legal fight with my mother, but fortunately it didn't come to that. Eventually they backed down. I had finally stood up to him. That is what I think people should do. Stand up for what you believe in. You CAN do it!

Yours, Daniel, 15, U.K.

Peace Child Inter
The White Hous
Buntingford
Herts, SG9 9AH
UNITED KINGDOM

Hi. I'm Sarah. When my parents went through a divorce, it was terrible. I hated watching my mother cry every day. She was trying really hard to keep the family together. The whole situation was very difficult.

Thanks for listening.

Sarah, 16, Canada

Child Internation.

White House

untingford

s, SG9 9AH

O KINGDOM

Peace Child International

The White Hou

Buntin

HERT

We know what jail is all about because our fathers were in there for so many years. They were put in for eight years for the same thing and we don't think it was that bad. We went to see them every Tuesday and we were always searched by the guards. They were very rude and listened to every word we said. When we had to say goodbye, it was very sad seeing our fathers go. We were only three when they went in and we think they should have been around to see us grow up. We were 11 years old when our fathers came out and it is much better now they're home.

Treasa Harking, 11, and Danielle Moore, 13, Northern Ireland

Peace Child International

The White House

Buntingford

HERTS, SG9 9AH

UNITED KINGDOM

I DON'T WANT TO HEAR ABOUT HIM ANYMORE!

I DON'T WANT TO HEAR ABOUT HER ANYMORE!

I used to be so happy at home—your average 16 year old girl, going to school and having fun. I had such a loving family. A caring mother, a wonderful brother and a responsible father. Now this man who I worshipped throughout my life has shattered all the faith that I had in him. Last month, my father told me that he was taking me on holiday to another country, just the two of us. I remember how excited I was. After we arrived at our hotel, he burned my passport and told me that he had arranged for me to get married in this country. I am so scared. I have never seen the man who is to be my husband and I haven't heard from my mother. Please help me. I have heard stories of other girls being married off and how badly they get treated by their "husbands." I want to go home to my mother.

Shabana, 16, U.K.

Peace Child International

The White House

Buntingford

Herts, SG9 9AH

United Kingdom

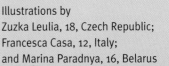

Illustrations by
Zuzka Leulia, 18, Czech Republic;
Francesca Casa, 12, Italy;
and Marina Paradnya, 16, Belarus

Education

Everybody needs education. Just think, if you hadn't gone to school, you wouldn't be able to read this book. In fact, you wouldn't be able to read any books, newspapers or the Internet. You would miss out on the chance to find out about the world. By learning at school, you can build yourself a better future. You'll be able to get the job you deserve and understand the world around you.

● The right to an education is so important that we've devoted a whole chapter to it.

● On pages 60–61, we investigate whether girls have the same rights to education as boys. We also ask what changes some of our contributors would make if they were the principals at their schools.

● The chapter also looks at what sort of education is needed for people to become informed citizens, including views on how children are disciplined at school.

Illustration by Nzuzi Matenkadi Giresse, 16, Democratic Republic of Congo

Articles in this chapter

Article 28 The right to education, including free primary education. Discipline to be consistent with a child's human dignity.

Article 29 The right to an education which prepares her/him for an active, responsible life as an adult in a free society which respects others and the environment.

Illustration opposite by Alejandra Otero M., 8, Peru

The Right to Go to School

What does education mean to you? How important is it to your future? As you read these pages, consider this: according to a report on the state of the world's children, more than 130 million children in developing countries are growing up without receiving a basic education.

Free education for all
The Convention gives every child the right to free elementary school education. Some governments complain that this is too expensive. But it would cost $8 trillion, the amount the world spends on the military in just four days.

Illustration by Srijana Shrestha, 17, Nepal

" *Girls have as much right to be educated as boys, yet in many countries, girls don't receive even a basic education. Attitudes are often formed at very young ages and parents are afraid that their daughters will become pregnant from meeting boys at school. In some areas of the world— like small towns in the mountains of Peru— girls are denied an education merely because the men and boys cannot respect that girls have a right to a 'life,' too.* "

Sara Encinas, a teacher from Peru

fact
According to the latest figures, 80 million girls between ages 6 and 11 don't go to school.

Boys and girls

*Boys and boys gather round
pens and paper all around
learn to write, learn to read
take this all turned into greed
have a job without a care
but in your bodies, hearts are bare
so while you sit and take in more
others perish on the floor.*

*Girls and girls gather round
men and orders all around
you're not allowed to read or write
your brilliant minds pushed into night
work all day not for your good
cook and clean, learn if you could
for you don't deserve the same as males
and are left behind in their trails.*

Poem and illustrations by Carmen Jungblut, 14, Canada

Thanks to UNICEF and the UN Department for Publications and Information for supplying statistics for this page.

Your education... your future

" In my country, I have to learn so many subjects to prepare for the most important exams of my life, the ones that will determine whether I am a professor or a farmer. I have to do six exams for graduation and three more for college entrance. We really have no choice. "

Thuy Anh, 16, Vietnam

" We are not being educated for the future, for our survival. We concentrate on 'words per minute' rather than deaths per second from hunger or AIDS. We should know how to maintain a healthy, stable environment but still prosper economically. "

Melanie Coulas, 16, Canada

So what would you do if you were principal of your school?

" I would go around the whole country telling parents about the benefits of educating their children, to increase literacy levels in my country. "

Akosua Asaah Tioum-Barimah, 13, Ghana

" I would set up education for the poorer children which would cost them nothing. Sometimes education is not about money but about good will! "

Anita Pernatasari, 17, Indonesia

" There would be meals for pupils which would be paid for by the government. Most important of all, there would be free school equipment for everyone. "

Maja Ruzinovska, 13, Macedonia

" I would make sure that some schools have low fees or no fees at all. That is my wish. "

Geraldine Lwantale, 10, Uganda

Illustrations by Francesca Lopez, 10, U.S.A.

Education for Life

The Convention gives you the right to an education that prepares you for life. The idea is that if you have an education, you will become a responsible citizen who respects others and the environment. Well, that's the theory, but how does it relate to what you learn in the classroom? What sort of education do *you* get? Does it prepare you for life? Here are some ideas from our contributors.

" *We are lucky in Pillcopata, Peru, as we have a very nice school and good teachers. What is really important for us and our community is that the education is appropriate. Here in the cloud forest of the Amazonian jungle we need to be able to grow things—not just to eat, but also plants that make us better. We learn about the plants our shamans, or doctors, use to cure about 70 percent of our health problems.* **"**
Students from Pillcopata School, Peru

▲ This is where we meet in Pillcopata to discuss issues affecting our community.

Bullies are mean to you, call you bad names and make you feel like dirt. That sure does hurt my feelings.

Tiffanee Cariaga, 7, U.S.A.

" *Sometimes bullies are bullies because they are jealous of you and don't know any other way to react to that.* **"**
Jessica Ward, 11, USA

Illustration by Patricia Avalós, 18, Argentina

Dropouts

If you don't go to school, how can you receive the education you need? Every year, 90 million children drop out of school. Why? There are many reasons. Some parents are poor and cannot support their children, so the children have to leave school and work full time. Others drop out because of family problems—they feel so unhappy that they can't concentrate at school. Another problem is bullying. Some children are abused and insulted by other students because they are different. Some children feel they are not listened to or valued as people and this can turn them against school.

Thanks to UNICEF for the statistic for this page.

Discipline

If there is no discipline in a school, the students spend so much time messing around that nobody learns anything! But if the discipline is too strict, children may be abused by the teachers. The Convention actually forbids any kind of corporal punishment—no one should be allowed to hit children. If you were in charge of a school, how would you keep control?

Discipline in school
They used to beat me with canes,
burning hot metal poles.
With all the knocks to my head,
my brain was full of holes.

Who could I tell?
Who would ever believe me?
This was my teacher,
he had full control over me.

The situation is different now,
while I watch my children at school.
They have brains crammed with knowledge
and I'm still a fool.

Jabran Ali, 14, U.K.

Illustration by
Makiko Suzuki, 18, Japan

Illustration by Patricia Avalós,
18, Argentina

❝ *The importance of education seems not to be totally respected by teachers. Some do not work hard at their jobs and seem to be in it for the money. They spend a lot of teaching time in the staff room reading newspapers and drinking tea. The teachers who do work hard tend to be too strict, even to the extent of beating pupils as punishment.* ❞
Temwa Roosevelt, 17, Malawi

Special Needs

There are articles in the Convention to help people such as refugees, children in care and disabled children with special needs. For example, refugees need assistance because many of them have no money, no home, and speak a different language. We should help them all to play full and active roles in our society.

- On the next two pages, you can read about the problems faced by disabled children. We were sent some great personal stories from young people whose lives have been changed for the better by their disabled friends.

- The chapter ends with a look at a child refugee's journey and the decisions that she or he might have to make. Amnesty International helped put these pages together. The journey we describe is based on real life accounts of refugees who have been forced to flee their homes. What would you do in their situation?

Illustration by Marina Paradnya, 16, Belarus

Articles in this chapter

Article 22   The right, if a refugee, to special protection.

Article 23   The right, if disabled, to special care, education, and training to help her/him enjoy a full life in conditions which ensure dignity, promote self-reliance, and a full and active life in society.

Article 25   The right, if placed by the government for purposes of care, protection, or treatment, to have all aspects of that placement regularly evaluated.

Illustrations opposite:
Top left: "Blind man walking" by Florencia Guanca, 8, Argentina
Bottom left: "Rights of boys and girls" by Nathalie Howell, 9, Costa Rica
Top right: "African child refugee" by unknown artist
Bottom right: "Everyone needs a heart" by Karina Alvares, 9, Argentina

We All Need Respect

The Convention makes a special mention about children with disabilities, noting that they should be able to live full and active lives, just like everyone else. As these contributions show, some disabled children live in terrible conditions. But if they receive love, respect, care, and opportunities, they can really make a difference.

" *I know an eight year old girl who is mute. Because she cannot speak, she suffers awful punishments. She doesn't go to school like her two sisters and she hasn't even got a first name. She is always naked because her mother doesn't give her clothes. The girl only eats when her sisters decide that they don't want food. Nearly all the time she is locked in her room which is dark and dirty.*

Once, I saw the girl playing on the lawn naked. I noticed bruises all over her body where she'd been beaten. Alone and afraid, she tightly hugged a toy watering can so she could feel loved. At the time I felt angry and sad. Some days later, I had a dream that she was my sister. I played with her and she was happy. She didn't have to hug a toy watering can because she had a family who loved her. "

Larissa Orellana, 15, El Salvador

Illustration by Patricia Avalós, 18, Argentina

Special Olympics ®

Special Olympics

Special Olympics is an international program of year round sports training and athletic competition for children and adults with mental disabilities. In the early 1960s, a woman named Eunice Kennedy Shriver started a day camp for people with mental disabilities. She saw that these people were far better at sports and physical activities than many experts first thought. So in 1968 she decided to organize the First International Special Olympics Games at Soldier Field, Chicago, Illinois.

Since then, millions of children and adults with mental disabilities have participated in the Special Olympics. In the most recent Games, there were 375 track and field competitors. The different sports that competitors take part in range from Alpine skiing, cycling, and track and field to speed skating. There are now Special Olympics programs in nearly 160 countries around the world. Their goal is for all people with mental disabilities to have the chance to become useful and productive citizens who are accepted and respected in the community.

A special child

We received a poem and photo from Brooke Brinsky and her friend, Justine Hirschfeld, about Brooke's little sister, Britany.

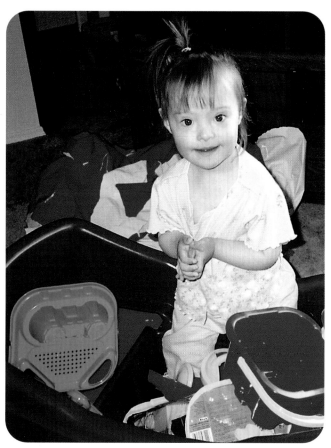

▲This is Britany, my sister. She's from Canada and she is two years old. She has Down's syndrome.

I am just a child. I need love too.
Just because I'm different,
doesn't mean you should care less for me.
When I do something small,
it means a great deal to me.
My life might be at a slower pace and less
flashy than others but
I help you slow down and see the things
that you take for granted.
The world has been blessed by special
people like me.
It's my destiny to reach out and touch the
lives of those who care for me.

Justine Hirschfeld and Brooke Brinsky, 11, Canada

❝ *Even though in medical terms I'm disabled, I really don't feel that way. I'm free to do what I like, when I like. Obviously going around in a wheelchair has some restrictions but it doesn't stop me from feeling like a normal person.* **❞**

Jenny Cook, 15, U.S.A.

Illustration by Melina D'Auna, 17, Argentina

67

Refugees: Put Yourself in Their Shoes

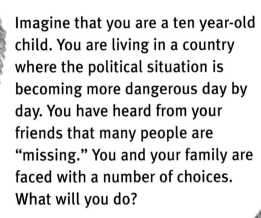

Imagine that you are a ten year-old child. You are living in a country where the political situation is becoming more dangerous day by day. You have heard from your friends that many people are "missing." You and your family are faced with a number of choices. What will you do?

Choice 1

Your father works for a newspaper and your mother stays at home to look after your baby sister. You have an 80 year old grandmother and two brothers. Your father has been receiving death threats and you hear that your lives are in danger.

Do you:

(a) stay where you are?

(b) hide with some friends?

(c) leave the country immediately?

fact

Last year, 7 million children became refugees due to natural disasters, wars, and abuses of human rights.

Choice 2

Your family decides that the only safe option is to leave the country and head for the border.

How do you get to the border?

(a) By train, although there may be police.

(b) Walk over the mountains for 12 days.

(c) Go by car and risk the roadblocks.

Choice 3

You decide to walk, but the journey will be difficult – especially for the old and the very young.

Who do you take with you?

(a) All your family.

(b) You leave your grandmother behind with friends.

(c) You leave your grandmother and your baby sister behind.

Choice 4

You hear that soldiers are coming to your house. You have ten minutes to gather your belongings together.

What do you take with you?

(a) Food, water and warm clothes.

(b) Passport and evidence that you are a genuine refugee.

(c) Photographs from your past and other personal mementos.

Thanks to Amnesty International and UNICEF for supplying the information and statistics for these pages.

PROTECTING RIGHTS

Amnesty International uses several different ways to make sure that people's rights are respected. Let's take a look...

Human rights education

Amnesty International members have put together a variety of education packets about human rights. They persuade governments to introduce human rights education into schools, universities, the army, and the police.

Working for individuals

Amnesty International supports individuals or groups of people whose human rights are being ignored. The Urgent Action network is made up of more than 80,000 volunteers in 85 different countries. They help prisoners and anyone in danger of serious abuse, such as torture or execution. They send e-mails, letters, and faxes to appeal to the governments of the world to take action.

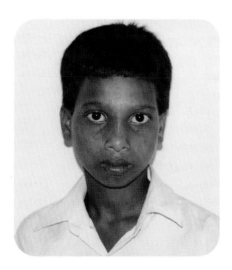

◄ In Bangladesh, the police arrested nine year old Firoz for stealing a mobile phone. Firoz was not allowed to see his parents. The police tortured him by binding him with rope and crushing his thumb with pliers. Amnesty International is working to ensure that this kind of incident is stopped.

Campaigning for human rights

Amnesty International brings the world's attention to people who are in danger of imprisonment, unfair trials, torture, or execution.

▲ An Amnesty International school group in Botswana carries out a successful letter-writing campaign.

Exposing the truth

Throughout the year, Amnesty International members visit various countries to sit in on political trials and carry out on-the-spot investigations into abuses of human rights. They produce detailed reports about the countries and point out problem areas.

Specialist networks

Amnesty International has networks of specialists, such as doctors and lawyers, who use their skills to help victims of abuses of human rights. Every year, on November 20th, the anniversary of the signing of the Convention, a Working Group on Children launches the Annual Children's Action. This is a project on a particular theme, based on the Convention.

"This abuse is still the world's secret shame, a dark reality ignored by governments everywhere. Most children suffer in silence, their stories never told, their tormentors never called to account."
Amnesty International report

◄ A theater group in Peru joins in a marathon to celebrate the launch of the Stamp Out Torture campaign.

Thanks to Amnesty International for providing the information and statistics for these pages.

Our Final Message

Well, this is the end of the book and we, the editors, would like to leave you with a few of our own personal thoughts. Writing this book made us think differently about the world. We hope that it makes you feel the same. So when you have finished reading, think about the world you live in and every day try to make it a better place. *Thanks.*

❝ *This book is aimed at children, but I think it would be useful for adults to read as well, for they are the ones who give or take away the rights of children.* ❞

Marina Paradnya, 16, Belarus

❝ *We can all promote children's rights, by reading about them, talking, and giving information to people every day. Perhaps if we show how children really live, then ignorance will disappear. Maybe this book won't change the real world, but we could make some lives better and I feel glad for that.* ❞

Patricia Avalós, 18, Argentina

❝ *I hope that this book will reach children all over the world and make them think long and hard—not only about the examples of gross neglect of children's rights in this book, but also about those happening around them. I'd love to hear the feedback that the book receives in different countries.* ❞

Gyanu Sharma, 18, Nepal

❝ *This book shows that there are young people who want to look after their own rights as well as the rights of others who are less privileged. There are lots of things young people can do if they go to poorer areas and see how children live there. Are they treated well? Do they need school books? It would be great if this book made people realize how important children's rights are.* ❞

Dana Shaddad, 17, Qatar

Illustration by Nicola Aquilina, 11, Malta

" This book will promote children's rights because first of all it is written by children for children and that speaks for itself. My hopes after having done this book are many. I want to be able to inform people of the seriousness of children's rights. Most of all, I want other children to understand that this is a very important topic and one that concerns each and every one of us. Without educated and caring children, there is no future. "

Zoe Hawkins, 15, Canada

" I have enjoyed working on the book hugely. I hope the readers have as much fun reading it as we had making it. Children face all sorts of abuse, not only from parents, but from siblings and friends also. The Convention is just one way of getting this message across. I hope people take notice of what we say. "

Gulizar Candemir, 15, U.K.

" Young people can do a lot to promote the rights of children, by drawing people's attention to children. Now I know that children are not helpless. They have the strength and capacity to protect themselves. My participation in this project proved this. Taking part in it was very important and interesting for me. Thank you for the opportunity. "

Vahagn Hamalbashyan, 17, Armenia

" Children are the citizens of tomorrow. They should be well informed. I am sure this book will change the social atmosphere. Having worked on the book, I myself feel enlightened and have more knowledge about child rights than before. It was a nice experience. Cheers! "

Vaibhav Dayal, 15, India

The Convention on the

Article 1 The Convention defines a child as a person under 18 unless national law recognizes that the age of majority is reached earlier.

Article 2 All the rights laid down in the Convention are to be enjoyed by children regardless of race, color, sex, language, religion, political, or other opinion, national, ethnic or social origin, property, disability, birth, or other status.

Article 3 All actions concerning the child should be in her/his best interests.

Article 4 The country has an obligation to translate the rights of the Convention into reality.

Article 5 The country should respect the rights and responsibilities of parents to provide guidance appropriate to the child's capacities.

EVERY CHILD HAS:

Article 6 The right to life.

Article 7 The right to a name and a nationality and, as far as possible, the right to know and to be cared for by her/his parents.

Article 8 The right to protection of her/his identity by the country.

Article 9 The right to live with her/his parents unless incompatible with her/his best interests. The right, if desired, to maintain personal relations and direct contact with both parents if separated from one or both.

Article 10 The right to leave and enter her/his own country, and other countries, for purposes of reunion with parents and maintaining the child-parent relationship.

Article 11 The right to protection by the country if unlawfully taken or kept abroad by a parent.

Article 12 The right to freely express an opinion in all matters affecting her/him and to have that opinion taken into account.

Article 13 The right to express views, and obtain and transmit ideas and information regardless of frontiers.

Article 14 The right to freedom of thought, conscience, and religion, subject to appropriate parental guidance.

Article 15 The right to meet together with other children and join and form associations.

Article 16 The right to protection from arbitrary and unlawful interference with privacy, family, home, and correspondence, and from libel and slander.

Article 17 The right of access to information and materials from a diversity of sources and of protection from harmful materials.

Article 18 The right to benefit from child rearing assistance and child care services and facilities provided to parents/guardians by the country.

Article 19 The right to protection from maltreatment by parents or others responsible for her/his care.

Article 20 The right to special protection if s/he is temporarily or permanently deprived of her/his family environment, due regard being paid to her/his cultural background.

Article 21 The right, in countries where adoption is allowed, to have it ensured that an adoption is carried out in her/his best interests.

Article 22 The right, if a refugee, to special protection.

Rights of the Child

Article 23 The right, if disabled, to special care, education, and training to help her/him enjoy a full life in conditions which ensure dignity, promote self-reliance, and a full and active life in society.

Article 24 The right to the highest standard of health and medical care attainable.

Article 25 The right, if placed by the country for purposes of care, protection or treatment, to have all aspects of that placement regularly evaluated.

Article 26 The right to benefit from social security.

Article 27 The right to a standard of living adequate for her/his physical, mental, spiritual, moral and social development.

Article 28 The right to education, including free primary education. Discipline to be consistent with a child's human dignity.

Article 29 The right to an education which prepares her/him for an active, responsible life as an adult in a free society which respects others and the environment.

Article 30 The right, if a member of a minority community or indigenous people, to enjoy her/his own culture, to practice her/his own religion, and use her/his own language.

Article 31 The right to rest and leisure, to engage in play, and to participate in recreational, cultural and artistic activities.

Article 32 The right to protection from economic exploitation and work that is hazardous, interferes with her/his education, or harms her/his health or physical, mental, spiritual, moral, and social development.

Article 33 The right to protection from narcotic drugs and from being involved in their production or distribution.

Article 34 The right to protection from sexual exploitation and abuse.

Article 35 The right to protection from being abducted, sold or trafficked.

Article 36 The right to protection from all other forms of exploitation.

Article 37 The right not to be subjected to torture or degrading treatment. If detained, not to be kept with adults, sentenced to death nor imprisoned for life without the possibility of release. The right to legal assistance and contact with family.

Article 38 The right, if below 15 years of age, not to be recruited into armed forces nor to engage in direct hostilities.

Article 39 The right, if the victim of armed conflict, torture, neglect, maltreatment, or exploitation, to receive appropriate treatment for her/his physical and psychological recovery and reintegration into society.

Article 40 The right, if accused or guilty of committing an offense, to age-appropriate treatment likely to promote her/his sense of dignity and worth and her/his reintegration as a constructive member of society.

Article 42 The right to be informed of these principles and provisions by the country in which s/he lives.

Note: The Convention has 54 Articles in all. Article 41 and Articles 43–54 are concerned with implementing the Convention and bringing it into force.

The Convention on the Rights of the Child was adopted by the United Nations General Assembly on November 20, 1989.
Summary by Save the Children/UNICEF

Useful addresses

Amnesty International (pages 86–87)
Amnesty International raises awareness about abuses of human rights and works to help those who are suffering.
Contact: 322 8th Avenue, New York, NY 10001
Website: www.amnesty.org
Email: amnestyis@amnesty.org

Casa Alianza (page 77)
Casa Alianza helps street children build new lives and protects them from abuse.
Contact: SJO 1039, P.O. Box 025216, Miami, Fl, 33102-5216 USA
Website: www.casa-alianza.org
Email: info@casa-alianza.org

The Child Labor Coalition
The Child Labor Coalition works to protect working minors and end child labor exploitation.
Contact: 1701 K Street, NW, Suite 1200, Washington, D.C. 20006
Website: www.stopchildlabor.org

The Children's Defense Fund
The Children's Defense Fund aims for children to have successful passage to adulthood with the help of caring families and communities.
Contact: 25 E Street NW, Washington, D.C. 20001
Website: www.childrensdefense.org
Email: cdfinfo@childrensdefense.org

Children Now
Children Now is an independent organisation working with the nation's commitment to children and families.
Contact: 1212 Broadway, 5th Floor, Oakland, CA 94612
Website: www.childrennow.org
Email: children@childrennow.org

Human Rights Watch
Human Rights Watch is dedicated to protecting the rights of people around the world.
Contact: 50 Fifth Avenue, 34th Floor, New York, NY 10118-3299
Website: www.hrw.org
Email: hrwnyc@hrw.org

International Youth Foundation
International Youth Foundation is an international organization dedicated to the positive development of children and youth throughout the world.
Contact: 32 South Street, Suite 500, Baltimore, MD 21202
Website: www.IYFNet.org
Email: youth@IYFNet.org

National Children's Alliance
National Children's Alliance's mission is to build a voice strong enough to give all children the opportunity to grow up healthy, educated, and safe.
Contact: 1612 K Street, NW, Suite 500, Washington, D.C. 20006
Website: www.nca-online.org
Email: info@nca-online.org

Below, we have listed some action ideas, as well as giving information about the website that accompanies this book—check it out!

Ribbon of Promise

Ribbon of Promise is dedicated to ending school violence by acting as a resource for communication, education, planning, and action.
Contact: 150 Seventh Street, Springfield, OR 97477
Website: www.ribbonofpromise.org
Email: info@ribbonofpromise.org

Save the Children (pages 34–35)

Save the Children is the U.K.'s leading international children's charity, working to create a better future for children.
Contact: 54 Wilton Road, Westport, CT 06880
Website: www.scf.org

SOS Children's Villages (page 54)

SOS Children's Villages offer abandoned, orphaned, and destitute children a new and permanent home, and prepare them for an independent life. SOS-Kinderdorf International is the umbrella organization, to which all national SOS Children's Village Associations are linked.
Website: www.sos-kd.org

UNICEF (pages 14–15)

UNICEF is the part of the United Nations devoted to improving the lives of children and implementing the Convention on the Rights of the Child.
Contact: Unicef House, 3 United Nations Plaza, New York, NY 10017
Website: www.unicef.org
Email: info@unicef.org

Five great action ideas

1 Conduct a survey in your school about "Speaking up" to find out whether you think adults are listening to you.

2 Write articles for your school magazine about child rights issues in your area.

3 Make a video about how the lives of girls and boys are different, to find out whether there is discrimination between the sexes.

4 Get in touch with Amnesty International and take part in their letter-writing campaigns to make sure that the law treats young people fairly.

5 Hold an art competition to see who can design the best poster that makes you aware of your rights.

www.peacechild.org/speakout

When we were making this book, we realized that there were many more ideas, organizations and stories than we were able to cram into this book. So we came up with the idea of making a website to go with the book, where you can access loads of extra information. This is what you will find when you log on.

● Links to lots of child rights websites
● Information about specific issues
● Resources for teachers
● News of upcoming events and campaigns

Peace Child needs you!

Interested in making a difference? Looking for a way to connect with the rest of the world? Well, maybe you should get in touch with Peace Child—the organization behind the making of this book.

▶ The office is run by a team of young volunteers from all corners of the globe. Laura, from Costa Rica, was responsible for organizing all the groups who helped to write this book.

FACT FILE

What is Peace Child? Peace Child is a non-profit making educational organization that was founded in 1981. The best part about it is that everything is done by young people.

What are its goals? Peace Child is all about the empowerment of young people, through music, theater, literature, and community-based action plans.

What does it do? Peace Child runs a number of educational programs about human rights, sustainable development and the environment. It encourages young people to become actively involved in all types of projects and at all different levels.

Where does it carry out its work? Peace Child has headquarters in Buntingford, U.K. It works with youth groups, individuals and schools in 120 different countries.

In the last six years, Peace Child has produced a number of books dealing with topics such as human rights, the environment and peace. We are planning more, so if you would like to take part in helping us make our next book, please contact us.

◀ These are some of our other books, including *Stand Up for Your Rights*, a book about the Universal Declaration of Human Rights.

Contact:
Peace Child International, The White House, High St, Buntingford SG9 9AH, U.K.
Website: www.peacechild.org
Email: contact@peacechild.org

Be the Change
Be the Change is a web-based program set up by Peace Child, which focuses on projects developed by young people aged 12 to 25. To find out more, visit the Peace Child website.

▲ This is Irina, who works on the Latin American desk.

If you are between the ages of 12 and 25 and you want to organize a project in your community, send a plan of action to the team of young people at Peace Child. They are trained to help you.

▲ Mathias from France helps youth groups to develop ideas.

Glossary

Aborigine A native person of Australia.

abuse Bad treatment.

Agenda 21 A United Nations document outlining a way for the planet to survive in the 21st century.

AIDS A disease that weakens the immune system and makes it difficult for the body to fight infections. AIDS is short for Acquired Immune Deficiency Syndrome.

apartheid A system used to keep apart people of different races.

billion One thousand million. One billion is written in numbers as 1,000,000,000.

bonded labour When a child is sold into slavery and in return, the child's family receives a loan of money.

bully When one person uses threats or force to make another person do something against his or her will.

campaign A series of planned actions designed to make something happen, such as a campaign to stop children from being physically punished.

child labor When children have to earn a living by working.

citizen A person who lives in or belongs to a country.

constitution All the basic rules and laws that are used to govern a country.

convention A legal agreement.

Convention on the Rights of the Child A United Nations document that sets out the rights that all children should have.

corrupt When a person is corrupt, they act dishonestly or illegally.

culture The traditions, beliefs, and customs of a group of people.

dictatorship Government by one person with absolute power. A dictator is often supported by the army.

disability The loss of physical or mental ability such as the ability to walk or see.

discrimination To treat people unfairly because of factors such as race or sex.

drug abuse When a person takes chemical substances that harm his or her body.

education Acquiring knowledge and understanding, often through schooling.

equality The same status and opportunity for everyone, regardless of factors such as race or sex.

gender The sex of a person.

globalization Bringing the world closer together by using new technology.

government The group of people that runs a country.

HIV The virus that causes AIDS. HIV is short for Human Immunodeficiency Virus.

Holocaust The mass killing of Jewish people during World War II.

human rights These are people's basic rights to freedom, education and justice.

immunize To make a person safe from a disease, usually by giving a shot.

Industrial Revolution A period in history where machines were introduced and industry grew rapidly.

landmine An explosive device that is hidden in the ground.

literacy The ability to read and write.

malaria A disease carried by mosquitoes. A person with malaria suffers from fever.

malnutrition When people do not eat enough healthy food.

massacre The violent murder of many people.

mortality rate The number of people who die at any one time.

nationality Belonging to a particular nation.

oppress To treat people unjustly so they feel overpowered.

persecution To keep on treating people cruelly or unfairly.

ratify To formally approve an agreement.

referendum A vote taken by people on a particular issue.

refugee A person who has been forced to leave his or her own country.

register To record an event on an official list, such as the birth of a child.

religion An organized system of beliefs, ceremonies and worship.

responsibility Taking on duties and accepting the consequences of your actions.

revolution The uprising of many people demanding political change.

rights The things people are allowed to do by law.

sexual abuse When one person forces unwanted sexual attention on another.

slave Someone who is owned by another person. A slave has no rights.

social security Financial help from the country to help reduce poverty.

street children Children who work or both live and work on the streets.

tolerance Accepting the beliefs and attitudes of another person even when they are different from your own views.

torture Causing great pain to another person to gain information or as a punishment.

tribal peoples Groups of peoples of the same race who have the same customs.

UNICEF An organization that works to give basic rights, such as health care and schooling, to all children. UNICEF stands for the United Nations International Children's Emergency Fund.

United Nations (U.N.) An organization of independent countries that promotes peace and international co-operation.

Universal Declaration of Human Rights A document that sets out the rights to which every person is entitled, including freedom from slavery and torture.

vote A way of indicating a choice, often at an election or a meeting.

Index